Flowers of Scotland

Flowers of Scotland

text by William Fletcher

colour illustrations by
Roger Banks

line drawings by
Scoular Anderson

Richard Drew Publishing
Glasgow

in association with
The National Trust for Scotland

First published 1988
by Richard Drew Publishing Ltd
6 Clairmont Gardens
Glasgow G3 7LW, Scotland

Designed by James W. Murray

The publisher acknowledges
the financial assistance
of the Scottish Arts Council
in the publication of this book.

British Library Cataloguing in Publication Data

Fletcher, Bill
Flowers of Scotland.
1. Scotland. Flowering plants
I. Title
582.13′09411

ISBN 0-86267-217-1

Set in Plantin Light by Swains (Glasgow) Limited
Reproduction and printing by Swains (Edinburgh) Limited

Contents

Introduction
A New Beginning

EIGHTEEN thousand years ago much of the country which we now know as Scotland lay buried deep under about one mile (1500 metres) of ice. And so it had been for two thousand years before that. Scotland was a cold, silent, lifeless, glaciated world. Plants and animals that had developed in the temperate periods between previous ice-ages had been frozen out of existence. The land was in the grip of one of the great ice-ages that periodically covered much of our northern hemisphere with perennial ice (and will, no doubt, do so again in the future, for ice-ages come in cycles).

Vast quantities of water were tied up in the ice so that the seas were 100 metres lower than they are today. Britain was firmly attached to the continent of Europe for there was no English Channel and very little North Sea; Ireland was part of the same land mass for there was no Irish Sea.

And then, for reasons unknown, a great thaw set in revealing the land below. As the ice moved it scraped the tops off our mountains so that they were now lower than they had been and the glaciers, moving at 50 metres per year, gouged out great valleys, creating such as Glen Coe and the Lairig Ghru. Some of these valleys filled with water and became the lochs of today, for example Loch Ness and Loch Lomond.

Although the glaciers disappeared relatively quickly (in 4000 years) from north-west Europe, the great ice sheet covering North America took much longer so that it was only about 8000 years ago that Britain's last link with Europe was cut off by the rising seas. Scotland took on its familiar shape as we know it today 6000 years ago with the Western Isles, Orkney and Shetland isolated by water from the mainland to which they had formerly been joined. The land which was exposed was grey, cold and barren. It was a blank page on which Nature was soon to write her story.

During the period that Scotland lay under the ice, southern England was tundra-like, resembling Alaska of the present day; the Mediterranean countries, including North Africa, had a climate very much like Scotland now. As the ice receded so gradually plants once more began the journey north from the more hospitable south — first lichens and mosses, then grasses and sedges and heath-like plants and, as the soil accumulated, trees — birch, pine, oak and rowan and their associated small plants. These trees reached the Highlands 8000 years ago. Plants moved in to clothe the hillsides, to invade the fresh-water lochs, to populate the seashores, to create the peat bogs and to raise the forests. In their wake came the animals — deer, wolves, foxes, hares, the golden eagle and the snowy owl. And then man.

About 5000 years ago the people of the New Stone Age crossed the narrow, shallow seas from mainland Europe to colonise southern England and then to move north. These small people, they were about 1.5 metres in height, were farmers and they used their flint tools, together with fire, to clear the forests.

Stone-Age Man was the forerunner of the invading races — Bronze-Age people, Celts, Picts, Romans, Angles, Normans and Vikings, who were to transform much of our countryside and the plants that grow in it. Only the plants of the highest mountains were to escape their impact; and even they were hit, very much later, by Victorian plant collectors who pressed them between sheets of paper and put them into drawers in museums.

But a rich flora survived and some of the more interesting are described and illustrated in the following pages.

Early Summer in the Lowlands

SCOTLAND lies between 55°N and 60°N latitude, i.e. not far south of Alaska and northern Russia. As such, it should be much colder than it is, but the North Atlantic Drift which flows from the Gulf of Mexico to wash our western shores has the effect of making our climate relatively mild, particularly in the western lowland areas, although the temperature drops sharply with increases in altitude. Again, although rainfall can reach over 4000 mm per annum in some of our most mountainous areas, in some lowland areas around the Moray Firth and in East Lothian it may be as low as 600 mm.

Scotland can be divided into three areas — 1 the Southern Uplands, with its smooth rounded hills, 2 the Highlands and Islands, where many of the mountain summits are over 1000 metres and some of the corries lie under ice all year round (Ben Nevis, the highest peak is 1347 metres) and 3 between these the Central Lowlands, bounded by fault lines that run from Stonehaven to Helensburgh on the north and on the south from Dunbar to Girvan.

In this section we illustrate a few of the flowers that appear in the Lowlands in early summer.

1   *Few-flowered Leek*

2   *Dusky Cranesbill*

3   *Sweet Cicely*

4   *Marsh Thistle*

5   *Globeflower*

6   *Rosy Shamrock*

The white flowers of the *Few-flowered Leek 1* can be seen in June in grassland or on roadsides. Each plant, however, produces few flowers, scattered amongst very small bulbs, all protected by a papery envelope in bud. About a dozen geraniums can be found in Scotland. One of them, the *Dusky Cranesbill 2* has deep purple, almost black, flowers. It is probably a garden escape and is usually found near houses. It may be seen flowering in May.

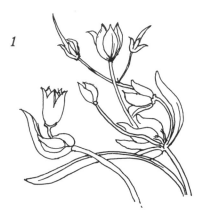

Among our earliest 'hedge parsleys' is the strongly aromatic *Sweet Cicely 3*. Its large soft leaves have white blotches. The small white flowers are grouped together in umbrella-shaped heads. The seeds are said to be used to flavour the liqueur, Chartreuse. The plant is an alien, being a native of the mountainous parts of Europe, but has become well established in Britain, especially in Scotland.

The *Marsh Thistle 4* produces its spiny leaves in the first year. In the second, its dark purple (occasionally white) heads are formed which, after fertilisation, develop a mass of silky down to form parachutes for the seeds. John Gerard, a 16th century physician, said, '"down" is gathered by the poore to stop pillows, cushions and beds for want of feathers, and is also bought of the rich upholsterers to mix with the feathers and "down" they do sell, which deceit would be looked unto'.

One of our most beautiful buttercups is the large *Globeflower 5*, flowering from June onwards in marshes. It is a pretender — the bright yellow 'petals' are really sepals, while the true petals are strap-like and function as nectaries. The little *Wood-sorrel* with solitary white flowers veined with purple, appearing in April, prefers dry woodland banks. A pink form, the *Rosy Shamrock 6*, can be found along the wooded shore of the Solway Firth.

Seaside Links in Summer

THE key plants in stabilising sand dunes are grasses, especially the broad leaved *Lyme-grass 1* and the narrow leaved *Marram grass 2*. Their long sharp-pointed shoots and the matted fibrous roots push out in all directions to bind the sand which is blown landwards by the onshore winds. Even when buried under a metre of sand these grasses can push up through it and soon establish the great rolling dunes. As the dunes are stabilised, other grasses move in to form the tough springy turf, the links so beloved of golfers. But they are also well liked by colourful flowering plants. One of the most noticeable is the ubiquitous *Common Ragwort 3* with its much divided leaves and bright yellow golden flowerheads. A very common weed of neglected or over-grazed grassland, it is highly poisonous to cattle and horses, although apparently not so to sheep. The caterpillars of the *Cinnabar Moth 4* don't find it distasteful either, since they feed voraciously on it.

Contrasting with ragwort are the long reddish-purple spikes of the *Rose-bay Willow-herb 5*. This is one of our most successful plants of recent years, having gained a firm foothold on the bombed areas (especially in cities) after World War II. It is also one of the first plants to colonise after grassland and forest fires. Little wonder that one of its common names is 'fireweed'. The main reason for its success is that it has two very effective methods of reproduction. It can spread by means of widely-creeping underground stems and it produces long narrow fruits containing masses of silken parachuted seeds which, in August and September, fill the air. The willow-herb is one of the few plants to compete successfully with bracken and in late summer many of our purple-coated hills owe as much to this plant as to heather.

On the links we note the delicate pale blue *Harebells 6* — 'the bluebells of Scotland'. These are widely distributed and may even be found at heights of 900 metres. *Hare's-foot Clover 7* — although fairly common on the dunes, is a rather unusual clover in that its creamy flowerheads are covered with fine downy hairs, leading to the common name.

Whorled Caraway 8 is readily recognisable by its whorls of fine leaflets. It is a plant chiefly of the western parts of Scotland, although it can be found in parts of Aberdeenshire. The seeds of a close relative, Caraway, are used for flavouring purposes, in particular the liqueur, Kummel.

Fluttering nearby is the *Meadow Brown* 9, one of the commonest European butterflies. The orange markings are particularly extensive in the forms found in northern Scotland. All round the Scottish coasts, parti-cularly where it is rocky or there are cliffs, we find the *Scots Lovage 10*. The small white or pinkish flowers are borne in clustered heads, characteristic of the family Umbelliferae (to which the caraways also belong). In times past, when fruit and fresh vegetables were not as plentiful as they are now, the leaves were eaten as a protection against scurvy. Great care had to be taken in identification, however, as a number of members of this family are highly poisonous.

1 Lyme-grass

2 Marram grass

3 Common Ragwort

4 Cinnabar Moth caterpillar

5 Rose-bay Willow-herb

6 Harebell

7 Hare's-foot Clover

8 Whorled Caraway

9 Scots Lovage

10 Meadow Brown

By Sea Lochs and Islands of the West Coast

THERE can be no more breathtaking scenery in the world than the west coast of Scotland from Cape Wrath in the north to the Mull of Galloway in the south. Over the sea to the Outer and Inner Hebrides, Bute, Cumbrae and Arran; the great sea lochs — Lochs Ewe, Torridon, Linnhe, Fyne and Long; and the mountain peaks of the Cuillins, Ben Nevis, Ben Cruachan and Ben Lomond.

Much of the land is moorland and among the moors we find orchids. Orchids are generally associated with tropical jungles so it may come as a surprise to find that we have eleven species in the Highlands and Islands.

Both of the *Butterfly-orchids 1* (Greater and Lesser) are so called because of their supposed resemblance to butterflies. In both species the petals are greenish-white in colour and they have a powerful fragrance, especially at night when they attract moths which pollinate them. Both prefer calcareous soils and may be found growing on hills up to 400 metres. The Lesser, which is more tolerant of acid soils, is more common in

1 Butterfly-orchid

2 Northern Marsh-orchid

3 Royal Fern

4 Burnet Rose

5 Northern Downy Rose

6 Rose-root

7 Sphagnum moss

8 Common Butterwort

9 Pale Butterwort

10 Round-leaved Sundew

the Highlands than the Greater. Another orchid, found on wetter soils, is the *Northern Marsh-orchid 2* which produces its spike of deep purple flowers in June and July.

The magnificent *Royal Fern 3* which can grow to a height of up to ten feet is, alas, becoming rare and is now extinct in many places where once it was fairly common.

A beautiful sight when it is in full flower in June is the *Burnet Rose 4*. Although the shrub itself is small (rarely over 30 cms) and very prickly, the creamy-white flowers are large, fragrant and, as they wither, produce attractive purplish-black fruits. It is common on sandy heaths near the sea and is found as far afield as the Outer Hebrides.

The *Northern Downy Rose 5*, so called because the leaves are covered with a mat of fine hairs, is a much larger plant, growing up to two metres in height. The pink, (sometimes white) flowers are more or less scentless. It has been recorded up to 600 metres in the Highlands.

The *Rose-root 6*, commonly found growing on sea cliffs and mountain crevices up to 1200 metres, is not related to the roses, but its thick root stock, from which the simple stem arises, is rose-scented. There are both

6

male (with red-tinged petals) and female (greenish-yellow) flowers.

Moorland peat, including bogs, is composed almost wholly of various species of sphagnum moss *7*. Some of these are able to grow totally immersed in water (squeeze them and they feel like sponges). Growing among the sphagnum we find two groups of insect-eating plants — the butterworts and the sundews.

The *Common Butterwort 8* has leaves which 'appear to be spread with butter'. They are actually covered with sticky glands which catch and digest insects. It produces beautiful deep violet flowers from May to July. The *Pale Butterwort 9* (pale, lilac-flowered) is a smaller, more delicate plant, but its leaves are just as deadly to visiting insects.

The leaves of *Round-leaved Sundew 10* are covered with bright red glandular hairs. Flies are attracted to these hairs which are very sticky. They bend over to completely enmesh this Lacewing which will then be digested by enzyme action.

4

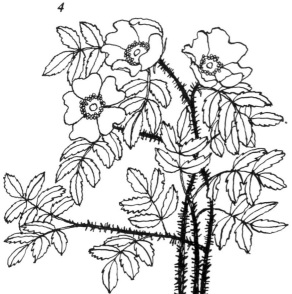

10

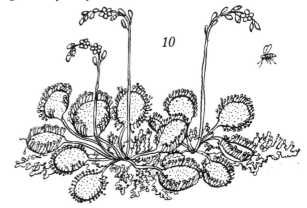

Flowers of the Loch and Bogside

WHEN the retreating glaciers gouged out the great valleys many of them subsequently became filled with water from the melting snows to form fresh-water lochs. Some have remained as such; others have been filled in by the growth of sphagnum moss to form great tracts of bog. Both loch and bog are found throughout the Highlands. In and around them we find some very attractive flowers.

One of these, the *Yellow Water-lily 1* is also called the 'brandy bottle' from the shape of its seedheads which reputedly smell of alcohol. The thick rootstock, buried in silt at the bottom of the loch, sends tightly-enclosed leaves and flowers to the surface of the water, which can be as much as five metres away. There they open to display their beauty.

Also raising its leaves (each with three leaflets like the bean, to which it is not related) and beautiful white flowers tinged with pink above the water is the *Bogbean 2*. Another plant of the lochs is the *Water Lobelia 3* with its submerged, narrow, hollow leaves and its small, pale blue flowers. It is very common on Speyside.

Floating on the surface of the lochs we note the oblong leaves of the *Red Pondweed 4* and its clusters of very much reduced flowers which give rise to small reddish fruits.

Bladderwort 5 is there too, free floating with its finely divided submerged leaves, bearing many tiny bladders which are traps for unwary water insects. If one should happen to touch the tiny hairs attached to the lid of the bladder the lid opens and the insect is swept inside to be digested. Bright yellow flowers are carried on stems above the surface of the water to be pollinated by insects.

Awlwort 6 is a small submerged aquatic plant. Rooted in the gravel of shallow lochsides, it is an annual, flowering from June to September. Submerged flowers usually remain closed and self-pollinate. Tiny white flowers above the water are insect-pollinated.

Pipewort 7, which has been reported from about twenty localities in the Inner Hebrides and the extreme west of Scotland, is the only European representative of what is mainly a tropical family. It may have found its way here from North America. It forms mats on the

margins of lochs or on wet, peaty ground. In the marshes and bogs we find *Marsh Cinquefoil 8*, so called because each leaf is divided into five (though sometimes seven) leaflets. The red-purple flowers are very characteristic. Also in marshy/boggy situations is the *Common Butterwort 9* which has already been described.

A common plant of mountain bogs and streamsides up to 1170 metres is the *Yellow Mountain Saxifrage 10* which produces flowers — bright yellow with orange dots — from June to August.

Red Rattle 11 (shake the seed pods to find out how it gets its name) with its deep red flowers and its much divided leaves, derives much of its nourishment by attaching its roots to the roots of other plants.

It was in the first century A.D. that the Greek physicians described a beautiful flower — white with yellow veins — growing on Mount Parnassus. And the *Grass of Parnassus 12* (though not a grass) is with us still and is common throughout marshes and moors up to nearly 800 metres. It smells faintly of honey.

1 *Yellow Water-lily*

2 *Bogbean*

3 *Water Lobelia*

4 *Red Pondweed*

5 *Bladderwort*

6 *Awlwort*

7 *Pipewort*

8 *Marsh Cinquefoil*

9 *Common Butterwort*

10 *Yellow Mountain Saxifrage*

11 *Red Rattle*

12 *Grass of Parnassus*

The Ancient Birchwoods of Loch Ness

AFTER the retreat of the ice the birches were among the first trees to invade Scotland. Although they are still very common, individual woods tend to be very small in area, probably kept in check by deer and rabbits. On sandy heaths small woods are found; on the mountains patches of woodland can be seen clothing the hillsides and individual trees cling to rock faces. Although the silver birch is common in southern and eastern Scotland the *Downy Birch 1* is more common in the Highlands. There are remnants of the ancient forest on the south shores of Loch Ness.

Within these woods there is no more beautiful sight than a bank of *Bluebells 2* in spring; and there is no more sad sight than great armfuls of wilted and dying bluebells being carried home by children — and yet many of us did it. Fortunately, the bluebell can survive such devastation and is not wholly dependent on its seed for spread; it is a wild hyacinth and, like its cultivated relative, it produces lots of bulbs underground. In woodlands the bulbs send their leaves above ground and produce perfumed flowers on long stalks before the trees come into leaf, thus gaining the maximum sunlight

1 *Downy Birch*

2 *Bluebell*

3 *Mountain Pansy*

4 *Wintergreen*

5 *Twinflower*

6 *Hairy Brome*

7 *Creeping Soft-grass*

8 *Heath grass*

9 *Chequered Skipper*

The *Twinflower 5* is a very rare plant, being found only in eastern Scotland, mainly in Aberdeenshire and Morayshire. It is a small creeping perennial which gets its name from the fact that each upright flower stalk bears two flowers. These appear from June to August. It has the distinction of taking its scientific name — *Linnaea* — from the great Swedish botanist, Linnaeus.

Various species of grasses are found in the birchwoods, including *Hairy Brome 6, Creeping Soft-grass 7* and *Heath grass 8.*

The bright green caterpillars of the *Chequered Skipper 9* eventually form pupae in silk-spun shelters made of leaves and hatch to give rise to the dapple-winged butterfly which appreciates the open birchwoods. Although this butterfly is found in the English Midlands, the Scottish variety is distinct with more heavily accented dark brown markings.

before shade closes in on them. The flowers are usually violet-blue in colour; more rarely they may be pink or even white. The bluebell is common throughout most of Scotland, but it is not found in Orkney or Shetland.

The Mountain Pansy 3 appears in a number of guises — yellow or purple, or sometimes a mixture of both. It is a common plant of open woods, hill pastures and moorland.

Three species of *Wintergreen 4* are to be found in the Highlands. They are separated mainly by the detailed structure of the flower, but the petals of *Larger Wintergreen* are white, those of the *Common Wintergreen* and *Intermediate Wintergreen* pinkish. Wintergreen oil is used as an ingredient of embrocations and lotions.

The Straths of the North East

THIS area, bounded on the west by Loch Ness and the Caledonian Canal, is dominated by the great massif of the Grampians. Among the many high peaks are Ben Macdui (1310 metres) and Cairngorm (1245 metres). The mountains are intersected by many rivers, among them the Spey with its outlet at Buckie, the Don and the Dee joining the North Sea at Aberdeen, the Tay and its many tributaries running south to Perth. All of them, and many others, run through the great wide, flat-bottomed valleys known as straths along which we find an array of plants.

The *Nootka Lupin 1* growing on river gravels is a native of Canada from Nootka Sound in British Columbia.

The *Tuberous Comfrey 2* with its bell-shaped yellow flowers is not a native either, though its home is probably Eastern Europe. It is an escapee from cultivation and was used as animal fodder. It is commonly found growing in woods on the banks of the rivers.

The *Melancholy Thistle 3* on the other hand, with its red-purple heads, is very much a native. In times past people believed that it was a charm against sadness and the 17th century physician, Nicholas Culpeper, recommended that a potion of the leaves in wine 'expels superfluous Melancholy out of the Body and makes a man merry as a cricket'. Perhaps the wine alone would do that!

Within the remnants of the Caledonian forest of *Scots Pine 4* are found some of our most interesting plants such as the *Lesser Twayblade 5* orchid. Each plant has only two leaves; the small reddish-green flowers are produced in great numbers on a long green stalk from June to August.

One of the commonest orchids widely distributed on the heaths and moors is the *Heath Spotted Orchid 6*, which can be found at heights up to 900 metres. The leaves are very commonly, though not always, spotted. The flowers, borne in a spike, are generally rose pink, but white forms may also be found.

One of our rarest plants is the *One-flowered Wintergreen 7*. Its solitary white flowers are to be found in the pinewoods.

The *Northern Bedstraw 8* is a fairly common plant of streamsides and shingle. The leaves are in whorls of four and the small white flowers give rise to brownish fruits which have hooked bristles to aid their dispersal.

The *Chickweed Wintergreen 9* is neither a chickweed nor a wintergreen. It is a close relative of the primrose. It is widely distributed among the moss of the pinewoods where its attractive white or pinkish flowers appear in June and July. These are borne in ones or twos on a stem springing from a whorl of green leaves.

The *Wood Cranesbill 10* with its attractive reddish-purple flowers belongs to the geranium family.

The juicy red *Raspberry 11* fruit is known to everyone and there are, of course, many cultivated varieties. The wild raspberry grows well in open woodlands especially on sandy soils. Interestingly enough the original English name was 'hindberry' — the berry eaten by hinds. How or when the name was changed is not known.

Another economically important plant is *Barley 12* which is included here to remind us that the seeds of this cereal are used both to fatten the world-famous Aberdeen Angus cattle and also, when malted, to produce the equally world-famous Scottish malt whiskies.

In these valleys too, we may see the *Scotch Argus 13* butterfly, which despite its name is common in Europe and east to the Caucasus and Ural Mountains. It will fly only if the sun is shining.

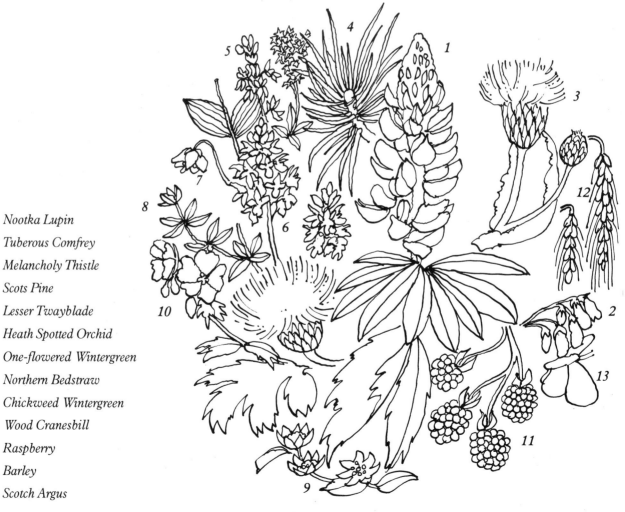

1   *Nootka Lupin*

2   *Tuberous Comfrey*

3   *Melancholy Thistle*

4   *Scots Pine*

5   *Lesser Twayblade*

6   *Heath Spotted Orchid*

7   *One-flowered Wintergreen*

8   *Northern Bedstraw*

9   *Chickweed Wintergreen*

10   *Wood Cranesbill*

11   *Raspberry*

12   *Barley*

13   *Scotch Argus*

The Northern Shore at Midsummer

LASHED by great waves and storms in winter, the northern coast, stretching from Cape Wrath to John o' Groats, shelters some of the most delicate and rare plants in summer. It is a fascinating countryside — miles upon miles of seemingly endless moorland, high peaked and menacing mountains showing great white patches of limestone rock, heath almost abutting the sea, great cliffs and sparkling silver white sand.

On the wet pastures and cliffs of northern shores of Sutherland and Caithness and in the Orkneys — and only in those places — grows the little pink-purple *Scottish Primrose 1*. A biennial or perennial, it flowers in May/June and again in July/August. It was first recorded in 1819 near Thurso.

Both the *Purple Milk Vetch 2*, a legume, with its paired leaflets and its dense clusters of purple flowers and the *Purple Oxytropis 3* with its characteristic, silky haired leaves are illustrated. The former is fairly common; the latter rather rare.

1   Scottish Primrose
2   Purple Milk Vetch
3   Purple Oxytropis
4   Small Blue
5   Pyramidal Bugle
6   Mountain Everlasting
7   Frog Orchid
8   Spring Squill
9   Oyster-plant
10   Glaucous Sedge
11   Sea Plantain
12   Moonwort

The *Small Blue 4* is one of the smallest European butterflies. Despite its name the females are brown, but the male has a scattering of blue scales on the upper side of its wings. The larvae feed on vetches and related plants.

A local species of the calcareous rocks in northwest Scotland and in the Hebrides is the *Pyramidal Bugle 5*. Its pale mauve flowers, half hidden by the hairy leaves, appear in May/June. The plant is shaped rather like a pyramid and 'bugle' may arise from the shape of its flowers.

The *Mountain Everlasting 6*, like its relative the Edelweiss of the Swiss mountains, is covered with a dense felt of white woolly hairs. The male (white) and the female (pink) flowers are borne on separate plants appearing in June/July.

A little imagination is needed to see the resemblance between the rather inconspicuous, greenish flowers of the *Frog Orchid 7* and the animal after which it was named. This plant likes limestone turf and it may be found growing up to 1000 metres.

Within reach of the salt spray of the sea grows the *Spring Squill 8*. The bluish bract below each violet-blue flower, appearing in spring, indicates that this is a close relative of the Bluebell (Wild Hyacinth). Unlike it, however, all the flowers of the squill are held at the same level, even though the flower stalks arise from different levels. The seed heads are depicted here.

On shingle and sand, where it enjoys the rotting seaweed, grows the fleshy, bluish-grey leaved *Oyster-plant 9*. The leaves have the tangy, salty flavour of oysters. In times past they were eaten either raw or cooked. The bell-shaped flowers are pink when young, becoming blue as they mature.

The *Glaucous Sedge 10* has grey-blue leaves too, but these are narrow and grass-like. It has male and female spikes of very reduced flowers which lack sepals or petals. Another plant with narrow leaves is the *Sea Plantain 11*, but its leaves form a rosette from which arises a tall, stout stem bearing a spike of greenish flowers.

The curious little fern *Moonwort 12* standing only about six inches high has only one segmented leaf bearing a short branched stalk which carries numerous small sacs in which the reproductive spores are found.

Arctic Alpine Plants of the Breadalbane Hills and Central Highlands

O N many of the Scottish mountains, at heights over 900 metres, we find the arctic alpine plants, named from the fact that some are found growing in the arctic wastelands, others in the high mountains of Europe, some in both. There are over 200 species belonging to many different families and they are all well adapted to the harsh, extreme conditions in which they live. In winter they are subjected to violent storms, hurricane winds and snow. The soil may be frozen for eight months of the year and it may be as late as June before the summits are free of snow and ice. The plants have four months to grow, produce flowers, be pollinated, set and disperse seed — and during this period temperatures may reach 100°F at midday and fall to freezing at night. At times the soils may be waterlogged and at others subjected to long periods of drought. Intense sunlight may suddenly give way to deep cloud.

Almost all arctic alpine plants are perennial, passing the winter in a dormant state, ready to make a quick start when conditions are right. Their bright flowers attract insects quickly; they are low-lying to protect themselves from the wind; and they have small leaves to prevent excessive water loss.

Some of the finest arctic alpine flowers (though most certainly not exclusively so) are found growing in the Breadalbane Hills and the Central Highlands. Ben Lawers is particularly rich botanically due to its basic rocks (mica schists). You do not, however, need to be a mountain climber to view some of these plants. The Cairngorm car park (the highest in Scotland at 670 metres) has small gardens laid out with plants from the mountain top. And if you want to go and see them in their natural setting the chairlift will take you to 1220 metres where a short walk will take you to the summit.

One of the most beautiful with its large purple flowers is the *Purple Saxifrage 1*. It is also one of the earliest, flowering from February through to May. It is found on basic rocks in the Highlands, Orkney, Shetland and the Outer Hebrides, ranging from sea-level to 1200 metres.

The *Mossy Cyphel 2* forms roundish green cushions up to one foot in diameter, which are covered from June to August with small inconspicuous yellowish-green flowers. It is found up to 1190 metres in the Highlands and the Inner Hebrides. A small evergreen shrub the *Mountain Azalea 3*, which is covered with pink flowers from May to June is fairly common throughout the Highlands at more than 1200 metres (and in the Orkneys at 400 metres).

A splendid *Emperor Moth 4* visits the flowers in search of nectar.

Two rather rare mountain willows are the *Net-leaved Willow, 5* a short compact shrub with dark green, prominently veined leaves, found growing on mountain ledges above 900 metres and the *Woolly Willow 6* which, as the name implies, is thickly covered with hairs.

The *Bog Asphodel 7* is widely distributed throughout

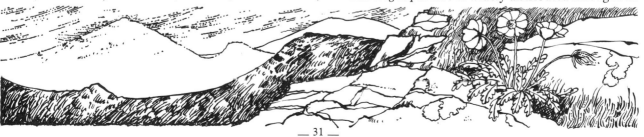

the peat and moorlands. Its bright orange spike of flowers gives a splendid splash of colour from June to August.

The *Mountain Avens 8* grow on basic rocks up to 1050 metres in the Highlands as well as at sea-level on the coastal dunes of our northern shores. After fertilisation the white eight-petalled flowers bear fruits with long feathery tufts of hairs which aid their dispersal.

The beautiful golden yellow flowers of the *Alpine Cinquefoil 9* make a splash of colour on basic rocks. They form a marked contrast with the bright blue of the *Small or Snow Gentian 10*. Flowering from April to September is the *Alpine Forget-me-not 11* with its small deep blue flowers. Here too we may find one of the thistles, the *Alpine Saw-wort 12* with its short tufted stem, its lance-shaped leaves which are grey and downy on the undersides and its clustered purple heads.

Two members of the legume family are illustrated. The slender *Alpine Milk-vetch 13* with its violet flowers borne in loose clusters and the *Yellow Oxytropis 14* with its rather tighter clusters of pale yellow flowers tinged with purple.

Rather inconspicuous is the small wiry *Alpine Meadow Rue 15* with its purplish petals and long drooping yellow stamens.

A fairly common plant is the *Dwarf Juniper 16* which is low lying forming almost a carpet growth. The fruits are berry-like, at first green then turning blue-black as they ripen.

1   *Purple Saxifrage*

2   *Mossy Cyphel*

3   *Mountain Azalea*

4   *Emperor Moth*

5   *Net-leaved Willow*

6   *Woolly Willow*

7   *Bog Asphodel*

8   *Mountain Avens*

9   *Alpine Cinquefoil*

10   *Small or Snowy Gentian*

11   *Alpine Forget-me-not*

12   *Alpine Saw-wort*

13   *Alpine Milk-vetch*

14   *Yellow Oxytropis*

15   *Alpine Meadow Rue*

16   *Dwarf Juniper*

Roger Banks 1971.

The Moors in August

MOORLAND is composed of very acid soils, low in minerals, with varying thicknesses of peat. Where the underlying soil is sandy and therefore well drained, it is known as heath; where the soils are waterlogged and there is a deep accumulation of peat, it is known as bog. A characteristic plant of the drier areas of moorland is heather. On the wetter areas there are great tracts of moorland grasses and sedges and, in the bogs, sphagnum moss.

Some 5000 years ago most of Scotland was covered with trees. Over the past 4000 years there has been a dramatic reduction in tree cover, so that today only some 9% is forested and more than 65% is moorland. Although Man has played his part in this, changes in

1 Heather

2 Bell Heather

3 Oak Eggar Moth

4 Bog Myrtle

5 Rowan

6 Creeping Lady's Tresses

7 Lousewort

8 Common Cow-wheat

9 Sneezewort

10 Spignel

11 Dwarf Cornel

12 Alpine Willow-herb

climate have possibly also been important. In late summer the moorland hills are ablaze with purple *Heather 1*. If you are lucky you may find a small patch of the white variety. Heather is not only decorative — it provides shelter and nesting for grouse; and food for both sheep and grouse. Patches of the very attractive, much larger-flowered crimson-purple (there is also a white variety) *Bell Heather 2* are here too. And feeding on the heather the *Oak Eggar Moth 3* which, in the north, takes two years to complete its life cycle.

In the wetter parts of the moor, where it may indeed be the dominant plant, is the fragrant *Bog Myrtle 4*. Crush the leaves and the aromatic fragrance is unforgettable. It was sometimes used to flavour beer and in the Highlands it was used in beds to ward of fleas.

On the hillsides the *Rowan 5* trees, with their masses of creamy white flowers which give way to bright red, glossy fruits in late summer, remind us that once, long ago, these moorlands were forests. And if we find the little cream-coloured orchid — *Creeping Lady's Tresses 6* — this will be a further reminder, because this rather rare plant is generally associated with the pine forest.

On the coarse grassland we find *Lousewort 7* which derives its name from the mistaken belief that it infested sheep and other animals with lice. It is interesting to note too that, just as the louse sucks blood from other living things, e.g. humans and sheep, so the lousewort derives water and mineral salts by attaching itself to the roots of other plants.

A closely-related plant, *Common Cow-wheat, 8* is also partially parasitic on the roots of grasses. The small yellow flowers are carried in the axils of the long narrow leaves. Despite its name it is not a cereal, but cattle are fond of it and it was believed that those grazing on it produced high-quality milk.

From July to August a common flowering plant on the moors is *Sneezewort 9*. It is so-called, says Gerard, 'because the smell of this plant procureth sneezing, hence Neesewoort'. Each flower (as in the daisy) is really a collection of flowers. The greenish-white flowers in the centre have both male and female organs, while the ray flowers (which look like petals) are female.

The finely-leaved *Spignel 10* is found as far north as Aberdeenshire. It is strongly aromatic and the cream-coloured flowers, borne in clusters on many-rayed umbels, give rise to egg-shaped ridged fruits. The roots are sometimes used as spice.

Growing among the heather is the *Dwarf Cornel 11*. The flowers appear to have four whitish petals, but these are really modified leaves. The true flowers which are purplish-black in colour, are to be seen in the centre of these leaves. By the streams, high on the hills, is the *Alpine Willow-herb 12*. Never more than six inches high, it bears fairly large pink, four-petalled flowers and like its larger relative, its seeds are spread by silky parachutes.

2

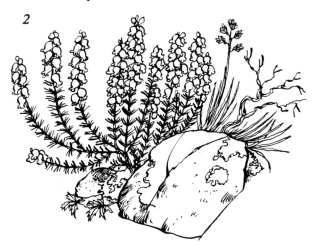

11

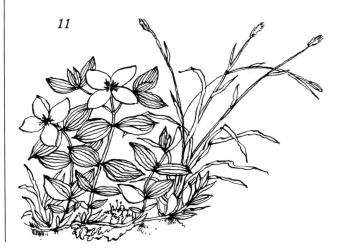

High Moors in Autumn

AS the days shorten and the temperature drops, so on the high moors many of the flowering plants set seed and form fruits. A few species may still be in flower, but soon they will follow suit. The club mosses, too, are producing their reproductive spores. Preparations are thus being made for the regeneration of life in spring, after the winter snows.

A common plant of the high moorland and bogs up to 1100 metres, with its head literally 'in the clouds' is the *Cloudberry 1*. Seldom more than six inches in height, it produces large white flowers from June to August. In autumn these give way to orange, raspberry-like fruits which are much prized by the Scandinavians in their countries, but are rather inaccessible to Scots in Scotland.

Blaeberry 2, after heather, is probably the most common plant of moorland. Its beautiful pink bells, which appear from April to June, yield delicious blue-purple berries which can be used for jellies and pies. The fruit of the *Crowberry 3*, however, is 'fit only for crows'. In May to June this small evergreen plant, found from sea-level to 760 metres, produces pinkish flowers with red stamens, followed by black globe-shaped fruits with 6-9 small hard stones within them.

The *Moss Campion 4* forms hemispherical cushions which are well able to withstand the high winds and the blankets of snow which it encounters on the mountain ledges at 1300 metres. From May to August each cushion is a mass of small pink flowers.

The *Clubmosses* are not 'mosses'. They are higher up the evolutionary scale, being more closely related to the ferns. They are remnants of the great group of plants (many of them attaining the size of trees) that clothed the earth some 350 million years ago, long before the coming of the flowering plants, and which formed our coal measures. They reproduce by means of spores. Three are illustrated here; the *Fir Clubmoss 5* in which the spore capsules are borne in the axils of the leaves;

the *Stag's-horn Clubmoss 6* in which the spore capsules are borne in cones at the end of long stalks; and the *Lesser Clubmoss 7*, a more slender species. All three are found throughout the Scottish mountains.

The *Autumn Gentian* or *Felwort 8* is widely distributed on dry pastures and also on coastal dunes. Its dull purple, or occasionally dull red, flowers appear from July to October.

Alpine Lady's mantle 9 can be found from sea-level (in Skye) to mountain tops (over 1200 metres). The small greenish flowers appear from June to August. A *Mountain Ringlet 10* butterfly, which is seen in flight only in sunny weather, is sipping the last of the season's nectar.

Both the *Alpine Bistort 11* and the *Viviparous Sheep's Fescue 12* grass have responded to the difficulty of producing seed during the short growing season at high altitudes by producing small leafy plants, or bulbils, instead of flowers. This is called vivipary. When shed these can take root and form independent plants.

1   Cloudberry

2   Blaeberry

3   Crowberry

4   Moss Campion

5   Fir Clubmoss

6   Stag's-horn Clubmoss

7   Lesser Clubmoss

8   Autumn Gentian or Felwort

9   Alpine Lady's Mantle

10   Mountain Ringlet

11   Alpine Bistort

12   Viviparous Sheep's Fescue

Scientific Names

Common names are used in the text. Scientific names of plants are from Clapham, Tutin and Warburg *Excursion Flora of the British Isles*, Cambridge University Press, 1981 and of butterflies and moths from Wilkinson, J. and Tweedie, M. *A Handguide to the Butterflies and Moths of Britain and Europe*, Treasury Press, 1986.

Note: Number refers to the Section in which the plant is illustrated and described.

10	Alpine Bistort	Polygonum viviparum
8	Alpine Cinquefoil	Potentilla crantzii
8	Alpine Forget-me-not	Myosotis alpestris
10	Alpine Lady's mantle	Alchemilla alpina
8	Alpine Meadow Rue	Thalictrum alpinum
8	Alpine Milk-vetch	Astragalus alpinus
8	Alpine Saw-wort	Saussurea alpina
9	Alpine Willow-herb	Epilobium anagallidifolium
10	Autumn Gentian (Felwort)	Gentianella amarella
4	Awlwort	Subularia aquatica
6	Barley	Hordeum sp.
9	Bell Heather	Erica cinerea
10	Blaeberry	Vaccinium myrtillus
4	Bladderwort	Utricularia vulgaris
5	Bluebell	Hyacinthoides non-scripta
8	Bog Asphodel	Narthecium ossifragum
4	Bogbean	Menyanthes trifoliata
9	Bog Myrtle	Myrica gale
3	Burnet Rose	Rosa pimpinellifolia
6	Chickweed Wintergreen	Trientalis europaea
10	Cloudberry	Rubus chamaemorus
4, 3	Common Butterwort	Pinguicula vulgaris
9	Common Cow-wheat	Melampyrum pratense
2	Common Ragwort	Senecio jacobaea
5	Common Wintergreen	Pyrola minor
9	Creeping Lady's Tresses	Goodyera repens
5	Creeping Soft-grass	Holcus mollis
10	Crowberry	Empetrum nigrum
5	Downy Birch	Betula pubescens
1	Dusky Cranesbill	Geranium phaeum
9	Dwarf Cornel	Cornus suecica
8	Dwarf Juniper	Juniperus communis ssp. nana
1	Few-flowered Leek	Allium paradoxum
10	Fir Clubmoss	Huperzia selago
7	Frog Orchid	Coeloglossum viride
1	Globeflower	Trollius europaeus
7	Glaucous Sedge	Carex flacca
4	Grass of Parnassus	Parnassia palustris
3	Greater Butterfly Orchid	Platanthera chlorantha
5	Hairy Brome	Bromus ramosus
2	Harebell	Campanula rotundifolia
2	Hares-foot Clover	Trifolium arvense
6	Heath Spotted Orchid	Dactylorhiza maculata ssp. ericetorum
9	Heather	Calluna vulgaris
5	Heath Grass	Danthonia decumbens
5	Intermediate Wintergreen	Pyrola media
5	Larger Wintergreen	Pyrola rotundifolia
3	Lesser Butterfly Orchid	Platanthera bifolia
10	Lesser Clubmoss	Selaginella selaginoides
6	Lesser Twayblade	Listera cordata
9	Lousewort	Pedicularis sylvatica
2	Lyme Grass	Leymus arenarius
2	Marram Grass	Ammophila arenaria

4	Marsh Cinquefoil	Potentilla palustris
1	Marsh Thistle	Cirsium palustre
6	Melancholy Thistle	Cirsium helenioides
7	Moonwort	Botrychium lunaria
10	Moss Campion	Silene acaulis
8	Mossy Cyphel	Minuartia sedoides
8	Mountain Avens	Dryas octopetala
8	Mountain Azalea	Loiseleuria procumbens
7	Mountain Everlasting	Antennaria dioica
5	Mountain Pansy	Viola lutea
8	Net-leaved Willow	Salix reticulata
6	Northern Bedstraw	Galium boreale
3	Northern Downy Rose	Rosa mollis
3	Northern Marsh Orchid	Dactylorhiza purpurella
6	Nootka Lupin	Lupinus nootkatensis
6	One-flowered Wintergreen	Moneses uniflora
7	Oyster-plant	Mertensia maritima
3	Pale Butterwort	Pinguicula lusitanica
4	Pipewort	Eriocaulon aquaticum
7	Purple Milk-vetch	Astragalus danicus
7	Purple Oxytropis	Oxytropis halleri
8	Purple Saxifrage	Saxifraga oppositifolia
7	Pyramidal Bugle	Ajuga pyramidalis
6	Raspberry	Rubus idaeus
4	Red Pondweed	Potamogeton alpinus
4	Red Rattle	Pedicularis palustris
2	Rose-bay Willow-herb	Chamaenerion angustifolium
3	Rose-root	Sedum rosea
1	Rosy Shamrock	Oxalis acetosella (*forma*)
3	Round-leaved Sundew	Drosera rotundifolia
9	Rowan	Sorbus aucuparia
3	Royal Fern	Osmunda regalis
2	Scots Lovage	Ligusticum scoticum
6	Scots Pine	Pinus sylvestris ssp. scotica
7	Scottish Primrose	Primula scotica
7	Sea Plantain	Plantago maritima
8	Small Gentian	Gentiana nivalis
9	Sneezewort	Alchillea ptarmica
3	Sphagnum Moss	Sphagnum spp.
9	Spignel	Meum athamanticum
7	Spring Squill	Scilla verna
10	Stag's-horn Clubmoss	Lycopodium clavatum
1	Sweet Cicely	Myrrhis odorata
6	Tuberous Comfrey	Symphytum tuberosum
5	Twinflower	Linnaea borealis
10	Viviparous Sheep's Fescue Grass	Festuca vivipara
4	Water Lobelia	Lobelia dortmanna
2	Whorled Caraway	Carum verticillatum
6	Wood Cranesbill	Geranium sylvaticum
1	Wood Sorrel	Oxalis acetosella
8	Woolly Willow	Salix lanata
4	Yellow Mountain Saxifrage	Saxifraga aizoides
8	Yellow Oxytropis	Oxytropis campestris
4	Yellow Water-lily	Nuphar lutea

Butterflies and Moths:

5	Chequered Skipper	Carterocephalus palaemon
2	Cinnabar Moth	Tyria jacobaeae
8	Emperor Moth	Saturnia pavonia
2	Meadow Brown	Maniola jurtina
10	Mountain Ringlet	Erebia epiphron mnemon
9	Oak Eggar Moth	Lasiocampa quercus
6	Scotch Argus	Erebia aethiops
7	Small Blue	Cupido minimus

Further Reading

THE following books may be found of interest. They are but a small collection of the many that are available.

The Alpine Flowers of Britain and Europe C. Grey Wilson and Marjorie Blamey, Collins 1979.
A beautifully illustrated guide to the plants of the Alps, Pyrenees and Northern Europe.
Ben Lawers and its Alpine Flowers various authors, National Trust, 1964.
Describes and illustrates the flowers from Scotland's treasure-house of Arctic Alpines.
Concise British Flora in Colour W. Keble Martin, Sphere Books 1972.
Invaluable for the quick identification of British wild flowers.
Discovering Wild Plant Names J. Stevens, Shire Publications, 1973.
Fascinating account of how many of our wild plants get their common names.
Field Guide to the Wild Flowers of Britain Readers Digest, 1985.
Packed with information, well illustrated, in a very pleasing format.
Handbook Guide to the Wild Flowers of Britain and Northern Europe Marjory Blamey & R. Fitter, Treasure Press, 1985.
A useful little book for identification of some of the common flowers.
Gerard's Herbal Edited by Marcus Woodward, Bracken Books, 1985.
The most recent edition of the work of the famous 16th century physician. Description and medical recipes for many common plants.
Highland Flora D. Ratcliffe, Highlands & Islands Development Board, 1977.
Written by the Chief Scientist of the Nature Conservancy Council. Beautifully illustrated by the author's own photographs.
Highlands and Islands F. F. Darling & J. M. Boyd, New Naturalist Series, Collins, 1969.
An authoritative book on the geology, climate, plants and animals, by two of our best known professional naturalists.
Plants of the British Isles Illustrated by Barbara Nicholson, Peerage Books, 1986.
Delightful illustrations of many of the plants of our countryside with a good text by Frank Brightman.
The Living Isles Peter Crawford, B.B.C., 1985.
Based on the recent T.V. series. Tells the story of the development of our plant life. Excellent and beautifully illustrated.
The Vegetation of Scotland Edited J. H. Burnett, Oliver & Boyd, 1964.
Produced for the visit of the British Association for the Advancement of Science in that year to Edinburgh. Comprehensive, but mainly for advanced study.
Wild Flowers of Britain Roger Philips, Pan, 1977.
Over 1000 colour photographs of individual species in this delightful book. A labour of love.
Wild Flowers of the British Isles I. Garrard & D. Streeter, Macmillan, 1983.
A beautifully illustrated book. The colours are dazzling and the drawings accurate. A collector's piece.

The National Trust for Scotland

THE National Trust for Scotland is a charity, independent of Government, promoting the permanent preservation of countryside and buildings of historic interest or natural beauty. In its care are over 100 properties as diverse as proud castles and humble birthplaces; lonely battlefields and beautiful gardens; mountains and islands.

Each year the Trust has to spend almost £8m to maintain these properties for the benefit of the nation and to provide the facilities for public enjoyment. The most important source of funding this expenditure is the subscriptions from its 160,000 members.

If you join the Trust during a visit to one of our properties, you can have your admission money refunded in full. As a member you will not only be helping to conserve your heritage but will also have free admission to all properties owned and administered by the Trust which are normally open to the public in Scotland as well as to nearly 300 properties of the National Trust, a separate organisation, in England, Wales and Northern Ireland.

You can join the National Trust for Scotland at any of our properties or by writing for details to our headquarters at 5 Charlotte Square, Edinburgh EH2 4DU.

Notes

Notes

Notes